They Wouldn't Quit

They Wouldn't Quit

Stories of Handicapped People

By Ravina Gelfand and Letha Patterson

Illustrated by Chet Sullivan

Medical Books for Young People

LERNER PUBLICATIONS COMPANY
MINNEAPOLIS, MINNESOTA

Standard Book Number: 8225-0013-2
Library of Congress Catalog Card Number: 62-16852

Second Printing 1963
Third Printing 1964
Fourth Printing 1967
Fifth Printing 1967
Sixth Printing 1969

CONTENTS

FOREWORD

People who have physical disabilities are sometimes called HANDICAPPED. But we really ought to find some new words to describe them. The biographies which you read in this book will tell you about fourteen successful people. They all had a special problem to overcome, but they did this so successfully that the term HANDICAPPED just seems inappropriate.

They all had a strong need or desire to achieve as much as possible, they had confidence in themselves and they worked very hard to reach their goals. Psychologists and other specialists who study human behavior are learning that a person's values and motivation are of utmost importance. When these specialists are asked to identify children or adults who are likely to be high achievers, they look for those who DON'T QUIT, for those who believe deeply in themselves and in the importance of their work and who keep trying.

All who read these stories will find them a source of inspiration, that precious quality which, perhaps more than any other thing, is the measure of one's handicap.

MAYNARD C. REYNOLDS, Ph.D.
Professor and Chairman
Department of Special Education
University of Minnesota

Chapter I

THE FLYING GENIUS

Alexander De Seversky

Russian-born Alexander De Seversky was a boy who enjoyed action—racing, diving, motorcycling, football—but airplanes fascinated him most of all. When his parents sent him to school at the Russian Naval Academy, he spent most of his free time around a factory where planes were being designed. Once in a while he was allowed to sneak a free ride.

After graduating, Alec went on to the Russian Military School of Aeronautics. It was then that he invented a special airplane ski which allowed Russian naval planes to continue in service during the winter.

When Russia entered the First World War, Alec became a navy pilot. One stormy night a group of the pilots were called together by their commanding officer. "German warships have been reported nearby," he said. "Who wants to volunteer for a bombing mission?"

Young Alec jumped to his feet faster than the rest. It was his first mission—a successful one—but in his determination to make good, he flew too close to his target. When enemy bullets hit his plane, he was forced to make a crash landing in which he lost his leg.

When Alec was able to get around on crutches, a job was made for him as an aircraft inspector. He had been grounded by his injury, but his mind stayed up in the clouds as he designed new equipment for the other pilots to use.

Soon, Alec was fitted with an artificial leg, and when nobody was watching he would get into the cockpits of parked airplanes to see how the rudder felt under a wooden leg.

One day Alec was supposed to attend a demonstration of new airplanes being held for high Russian officials. One of the planes at this air show caught everyone's eye. It was an ordinary airplane, but it was doing very extraordinary tricks. As the spectators cheered, the plane landed, and out stepped the pilot —one-legged Alexander De Seversky.

Now, Alec was in trouble—he had taken the plane up without permission. His commanding officer confined him to quarters. But when Czar Nicholas II heard the story, he had Alec restored to flying duty at once. Within one year after he had lost his leg. he was back at the front, downing thirteen enemy planes and proudly exhibiting a chest full of medals.

In 1918, Alec came to work in America as a test pilot. Although not yet a citizen the American government recognized his genius and appointed him a consulting engineer to the United States Air Force. His special assignment was to perfect a bomb sight. Within three years he had developed one that was 100 per cent accurate. Later he organized his own company to design and build planes. He married an American girl, became a naturalized citizen and joined the United States Army Air Corps Reserve.

The list of things one-legged Alexander De Seversky has accomplished is long and impressive. He designed a sea-plane which set a world speed record; he invented folding landing gears, wing flaps and many other things to make flying easier and safer. He broke many speed records and won world-wide honors. One was the United States Medal for Merit for his efforts in World War II. President Harry Truman, who presented the award, said Alexander De Seversky helped America win the war.

Alec never gave up when he believed in something. In the 1930's and 1940's he gave speech after speech and wrote books and articles trying to convince the people of the United States to build a more powerful Air Force. Many people did not agree with him, but he kept arguing and writing until he was finally taken seriously.

Fighting to retain his pilot's licence or arguing for what he believes is right, Alexander De Seversky is a man of courage. He lost his leg but always refused to stay grounded. He is still serving his adopted country—writing articles on aviation and working with the United States Air Force Historical Foundation.

Chapter II

Paul Wittgenstein

HE PLAYED MUSIC FOR THE LEFT HAND ALONE

It was not surprising that Paul Wittgenstein wanted to make music his career. Born in Vienna, Austria, of a family of music lovers, Paul lived in a home that was famous for parties where great musicians came to play. One of these was Paul's great uncle, the famous Josef Joachim, whom young Paul was permitted to accompany on the piano.

Paul was fortunate to have two great music teachers. One was a man named Teodor Leschetizky, "the maker of great pianists," who taught Paderewski and Schnabel. The other teacher was the well-known blind organist and composer, Josef Labor. When he gave his first big concert, at the age of twenty-six, music critics agreed that Paul Wittgenstein had great ability.

Paul's career was just beginning when World War I broke out, and the young pianist put his music aside to join the Austrian army. As he fought at the Russian front, he dreamed of the time when the war would be over and he could return to his beloved piano.

But soon it appeared that Paul's dream could never come true. Fighting on the Russian front, his right arm was shattered by a bullet. Before he could recover consciousness he was taken prisoner of war. In the prison hospital, the doctors had to amputate his arm to save his life.

He was sent from one hospital to another and finally to a large prison camp in Siberia. Over and over he thought: *this is the end of all my plans for the future.* But Paul Wittgenstein's courage and his love of music were too great for him to stay defeated. He didn't know how he would do it, but he made himself a promise: playing the piano would always be his greatest interest in life.

When he was sent home to Vienna as part of a prisoner exchange agreement, he started right to work. With aching fingers he practiced seven hours a day, and as each day went by the music he played with his one hand sounded more like it was being played with two.

Besides having to make one hand do the work of two, Paul was faced with another problem—there was almost no serious music written for the left hand alone. He spent months in libraries and music stores looking for pieces that could be arranged for left-handed playing without changing the music itself.

Finally Paul Wittgenstein gave his first one-armed piano concert. He used his forefinger and his left thumb to play the melody of the right hand. Since he was unable to play the upper and lower notes of a chord at the same time with his only hand, he broke the chord up. But the listener couldn't notice the break. By holding the chords with the pedal in a special way, he gave the impression of playing the whole chord at once.

At the end of that first recital the critics agreed that Paul Wittgenstein was a true artist. Many composers, moved by his courage, began to write original works of music for him. Richard Strauss, Sergei Prokofieff, Maurice Ravel, Paul Hindemith and Benjamin Britten were among them. It was the first time concert piano music had been written for the left hand alone.

In the United States, Paul Wittgenstein enjoyed the same success he had in Europe. In 1938 he brought his wife and three children to New York to live. There, in addition to concert work, he taught piano. Many of his pupils had only one arm.

After his seventieth birthday he made two long-playing records: *Paul Wittgenstein Plays Piano Music For The Left Hand*

and *Transcriptions For Piano Left Hand.*

A one-armed pianist might have enjoyed fame for a few years simply because people were curious or kind-hearted. But this kind of fame would not have lasted. Up to the time he died, in 1961, after more than forty years of concert playing, Paul Wittgenstein was considered a great artist—not because he played with one arm, but in spite of it.

NOTE:
Piano students interested in trying music written for the left hand alone may find some of the following available through music stores or directly from the publishers:

School For The Left Hand, a three-volume work of exercises and pieces arranged by Paul Wittgenstein, published by Universal Edition, London.

Sextet From Lucia, arranged for the left hand by Leschetizky, published by the Willis Music Company.

Digest Of Pieces For Left Hand Alone, published by Boston Music Company.

Five Pieces For Left Hand Alone, written by C. W. Krogmann, published by G. Schirmer, Inc., New York.

Old Black Joe, arranged by G. P. Maxim, published by the Boston Music Company.

Bonnie Eloise, arranged by G. P. Maxim, published by the Boston Music Company.

Chapter III

Glenn Cunningham

THE RUNNER WITH THE SCARRED LEGS

Who would ever think that a badly burned little eight-year-old boy, whose legs seemed permanently damaged, would grow up to run a mile faster than it had ever been done before? That happened to Glenn Cunningham.

Glenn lived on a farm in Kansas. To help pay for their books, Glenn and his older brother would get to the country schoolhouse early to build the fire before the other children arrived.

One morning, after filling the pot-bellied stove with wood, the kerosene was poured on and the match was lighted. But, by mistake, the delivery man had filled the kerosene can with gasoline. The stove exploded. Glenn's legs were badly burned.

It was weeks before Glenn could try to get out of bed. The toes on his left foot were almost gone and the shape of that foot was flattened. His right leg had been made crooked by the burns.

The doctor didn't think he could save Glenn's legs, but the boy and his family made up their minds to attempt the impossible. Glenn's mother and father massaged his legs by the hour, and then Glenn would work on them.

The first day that Glenn went outdoors on his crutches, the kids, who had been alerted for this big occasion, all stopped their play. They knew how hard it would be for Glenn not to be able to join in their running games.

Glenn noticed this and kidded them about it, saying they needed the practice—because someday he would beat them.

It took four years of massaging before the stiffness left Glenn's right leg. Then the doctor said that if Glenn could manage to run, the exercise might help straighten his legs and bring back some of the lost strength. So run he did. In fact, he hardly ever walked. He would still be running when his friends were all tired out.

At thirteen, Glenn made good his boast to beat the other kids.

"I'll race you down to the old oak," became "I'll beat you over the finish line," as Glenn competed at county fairs and Fourth-of-July picnics. He won a silver cup and several medals.

When Glenn went to high school, his friends and neighbors were so proud of him that twice they collected money to send him to Chicago to run in nation-wide contests. On the second try, he ran the mile in four minutes, 27 seconds, a world's record for high school runners.

All the while Glenn had been going to school, he helped out the family finances, working in the wheat fields and granaries. The work was back-breaking, but it made Glenn very strong. When he entered the University of Kansas, the track coach recognized that Glenn's great strength together with his courage and strong heart and lungs would make up for his lack of normal legs. The coach predicted that Glenn would be one of the greatest runners in history.

He was right. Glenn set a new American track record, and was chosen to represent the United States in the Olympic games. One year he won twenty-five out of twenty-seven races, here and abroad. And in his senior year, he ran the fastest mile: four minutes and 6.7 seconds, a record he later broke again when he went on to New York University. Glenn now has a ranch in Kansas where he invites underprivileged children to spend the summer. In the winter, he gives much of his time to youth activities and his special interest is the problems of handicapped children.

Glenn's legs never did become normal. But the sportswriters all agreed that Glenn Cunningham, breaker of world's records, was one of the greatest runners of all time.

Chapter IV

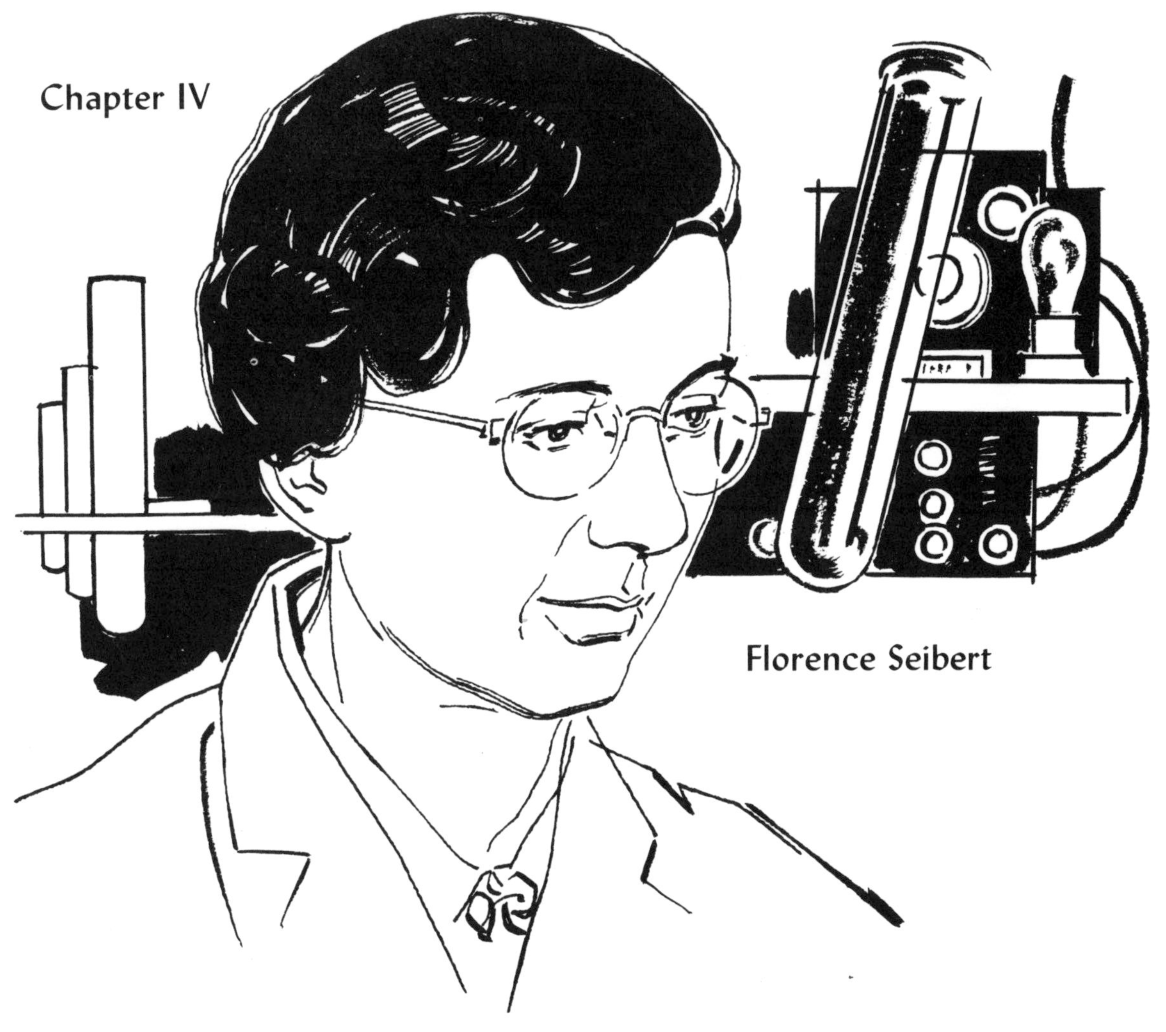

Florence Seibert

PIONEER WOMAN SCIENTIST

From the time she was a little girl, Florence Seibert played doctor. If she couldn't get her younger sister, Mabel, to hold still for bandaging, she would make a sling for her doll's arm.

Florence knew about doctors and doctoring. She had an uncle who was a physician. When he came to visit, Florence delighted in peeking in his black bag and playing with his stethoscope. And when she was three years old she had become ill with polio. She recovered, but she was left with a lame leg.

Florence wanted to be a doctor—unusual for a girl in the 1900s. As she grew older she realized that her chances of becoming a doctor might not be very good—doctors have to do a lot of rushing about and stair climbing.

Still, Florence didn't become discouraged. Her family never treated her as if she were different than anyone with two good legs. And she herself didn't feel any different. In fact, she usually forgot she was handicapped and didn't think about it unless she happened to catch sight of herself limping past a mirror.

Of course, Florence couldn't do some of the things the other girls did, such as hiking. But she enjoyed reading and studying, and this kept her from feeling left out. It also helped her earn a scholarship for a college education.

When she started college, Florence still thought about becoming a doctor. She wanted to help people by fighting disease. But her friends and teachers convinced her that being a doctor would be very hard for a person with a lame leg. And Florence realized that even if she weren't a doctor she could make a career of fighting disease. She became a *biochemist.*

Florence was really a pioneer woman because she became a scientist when few women were even getting a college education. She studied at three universities. It was at the University of Chicago that she was asked to help develop a better test for tuberculosis. At one time tuberculosis killed more people in America than any other disease. Today it kills far fewer people, thanks in part to the work of Florence Seibert.

Almost everyone knows about the Mantoux test—the little "mosquito bite" injection in the forearm which tells if a chest x-ray is needed. This is the test Florence worked on. Scientists had been trying to improve it for years, because it didn't always work right. For example, it might show a sick person to be well. Or, now and then a healthy person would take the test and the results would indicate he was very sick with tuberculosis.

There was something in the testing liquid that didn't belong there. And Florence had to figure out what it was.

It wasn't easy. The extra material was too small to be seen—and they didn't have the very powerful microscopes and other delicate instruments which we have today.

Florence worked for years. She even went to Sweden for a year to learn some new ideas from scientists there. It was hard work, but it was wonderful and exciting, too. And after ten years she succeeded! At last the Mantoux test could be trusted to give true results.

Now Florence Seibert is a retired professor from the University of Pennsylvania, but she still helps young researchers who are working to wipe out tuberculosis.

Florence Seibert had a physical handicap. She was a woman working in a man's field. She had to do a tough job without the proper tools. But none of these things stopped her. She set out to help fight disease—and she did.

Chapter V

James Thurber

HE FOUND HUMOR EVERYWHERE

Millions of people throughout the world have loved the special funny way James Thurber looked at life.

Born in Columbus, Ohio, on December 8, 1894, Thurber became a cartoonist, playwright and the author of twenty-five books and hundreds of stories and articles. Blind in one eye since the age of seven, he was a man who might have found much to be unhappy about. Instead he laughed and the world laughed with him.

Thurber was a newspaper reporter until he went to work for *The New Yorker* magazine in 1927.

His co-workers at the magazine, and his other friends were kept constantly laughing at his humorous pranks and tales. They especially delighted in the stories about the Thurber family, which James acted out, taking the parts of all members, including the dogs. In 1933 he began writing these stories, and many of them have been reprinted in books.

The relatives Thurber wrote about were very funny people. In "The Car We Had To Push" he told how his mother thought it was dangerous to drive a car without gasoline, because it "fried the valves or something." "Now don't you dare drive all over town without gasoline!" she would say. She also was afraid that the victrola (phonograph) was one of Thomas Edison's dangerous experiments that would blow up any minute.

Thurber explained that his mother got that way from her mother who suspected that invisible electricity was dripping all over the house. She thought it leaked out of empty sockets if the wall switch had been left on, and went around screwing in bulbs. If they lighted up she would be sure that she had saved the family from a dangerous electricity leak.

Thurber also liked to write about the family dogs. There were over fifty of them, the most famous of which is probably the Airedale, Muggs, who bit everybody except Thurber's mother. He said his mother used to send a box of candy every Christmas to the people the Airedale bit, and the list finally contained forty names. Since Muggs bit anyone who reached toward the floor, his food had to be put on top of an old kitchen table, and Muggs would stand on a bench and eat.

Besides his writing, Thurber is known for his unusual style of drawing which looks like doodling. He often said that when his cartoons first appeared in *The New Yorker* magazine, many mothers, thinking that Thurber must be a child, sent in drawings done by their children, claiming they were better than his. But his drawing achieved world-wide popularity. In his two books of fables, the strange-looking animals talk and act like people everyone knows.

While James Thurber was bringing laughter to others, he endured much suffering. By 1941, after a long period of trouble with his one good eye, he could no longer see well enough to use a typewriter. When five operations did not help his vision, he began writing with a crayon on yellow paper. But his eyes became weaker and he had to write larger and larger. Soon twenty words filled a page and a hundred used up the crayon. Only his wife and two secretaries could figure out what he had written.

Then he trained himself to give dictation. It was harder for him than it would be for many writers because so much of his work depended on using exactly the right word in the right place. To get his stories the way he wanted them he would write the text in his mind, shifting words around. By the time he called a secretary to type the work, he had sometimes remembered as many as three complete versions of the same story.

During the time he was going blind, Thurber wrote, among other things, two books for children in the third through the sixth grade. *Many Moons* is the story of a little princess who wanted the moon, and how she got it. *The Great Quillow,* is the story of the tiny toy-maker who saved his town from a giant.

When he became almost totally blind, Thurber had to stop drawing cartoons. But he kept writing, and his writing became even better than before because he concentrated completely on words. He had great fun playing with words—the way they sounded and the many different ways they could be used. When the available words didn't fit what he wanted to say, he made up his own.

James Thurber died on November 2, 1961, but the work he left behind will continue to make people laugh for many years to come.

Chapter VI

Leo (Bud) Daley

THE YANKEE PITCHER WHO DID THE IMPOSSIBLE

In July of 1961, one of the pitchers in a series between the New York Yankees and the Baltimore Orioles was left-handed Leo (Bud) Daley. He was pitching for the Yankees, and he had two reasons for wanting to win.

First, Bud was new to the team that season, and wanted to be named a regular starting pitcher. Second, the game was one of the year's most important, since the Yankees and the Orioles were among the top teams in the league.

Bud did win the game, and New York fans cheered wildly.

Few of them knew that the man they were cheering was once so deformed that it was considered impossible for him ever to lead a normal life. Nor could they tell that they had seen a game pitched by a man whose right arm is an inch shorter than his left, and who cannot even raise his right hand over his head.

Bud lost the use of his right arm through an injury at birth, and though his mother massaged the arm day after day, it did not seem as if he could ever use it. As a baby, Bud couldn't crawl because he had no way to support himself.

But neither Bud nor his mother would give up. By constantly trying to move the arm, Bud began to get some control over it. His mother bought him a set of weights to lift, and slowly the damaged muscles began to strengthen.

For years Bud Daley stood on the side lines watching the other kids play baseball, wishing he could be one of them. In his early teens this wish came true—Bud's determination had brought results and his arm was getting strong. At fifteen he was on the American Legion junior team and two years later was the star pitcher for his high school team in Long Beach, California. Several big league scouts offered him bonus payments if he would sign a contract to play with their team. The Cleveland Indians finally got him.

He was sent to the minor leagues for experience and for five years he pitched for last-place teams. It was very discouraging, because a pitcher has a difficult time earning a good record with a poor team. Finally, in 1956, he led the Indianapolis team to the American Association championship by winning eleven games and losing only one. He won two more games in the playoffs and was named Indianapolis' most valuable player.

Bud got his big league chance in 1957 at Cleveland, but won only two games and lost ten. He had married his high school sweetheart, Dorothy Mae Olson, in 1952, and had four children to cheer for him by the time he was making a name for himself with the Kansas City Athletics. In 1959 he won sixteen games for Kansas City, a team which finished next to last. A pitcher who wins sixteen games for a poor team compares with one who wins more than twenty games for a leading team. The following year he won sixteen games again for Kansas City, which this time finished in last place.

Both in 1959 and 1960, Bud was picked to play for the American League in the All-Star game against the National League's best players. In 1961 when the Yankees badly needed an experienced pitcher, the man they wanted was Bud Daley. To obtain him in a trade with Kansas City, the Yankees gave two players—a pitcher who had won fifteen games and a promising young catcher.

The Yankees not only received an outstanding pitcher in Daley—they also added to their team one of the best hitting and fielding pitchers in baseball. Because Bud cannot twist his right arm in all positions, he has to field most balls backhanded: that is, with the back of his hand turned toward himself. He does this so well that he made only one error in 1961. In fact, he is so quick and skillful most fans fail to see that he always backhand catches the return throw from the catcher.

Bud Daley's birth injury pinched the nerve that controls his right arm. But American League hitters say that Leo (Bud) Daley controls the baseball as well as any pitcher in the game.

Chapter VII

Kate Smith

BORN TO SING

Kate Smith was born to sing. She had such a perfect sense of pitch that she could tell when one player, out of an entire orchestra, played a wrong note. She never took singing lessons and she never learned to read music—she learned "by ear."

Kate was a happy girl and as she went about her work or play she would hum, or break out with a new song that she had just learned. She always enjoyed the family get-togethers, particularly at holiday time, when her grandparents would come and everyone gathered around the piano to sing old favorites.

At the age of fourteen, Kate developed gland trouble which caused her to gain weight. As she got fatter and fatter, the children at school began to tease her. Kate was so upset that she no longer wanted to play with them. She would hurry home from school, shut herself in her room and cry.

Kate Smith had a natural love for people and it just wasn't like her to spend so much time alone. Her grandmother urged her to forget about being fat and concentrate on developing her lovely voice.

Kate took her grandmother's advice, and before long she was winning prizes at the amateur nights put on by the local theater in Washington, D. C., where she lived.

More than anything else, Kate wanted to become a professional singer. Her parents thought it would be better if she studied nursing. They thought her huge size was too much of a handicap for her to be successful on the stage.

So Kate started nurses' training, but all the while she longed to be singing instead. Finally she decided to forget about being a nurse. In her heart she believed that people would forget her looks when they heard her voice.

At first it seemed that Kate was wrong.

She went to Broadway where she got a small part in a musical comedy. She sang and danced beautifully, but she was cast with a man whose part called for him to make fat-girl jokes.

The jokes brought down the house with laughter. Kate was deeply hurt inside. She knew it wasn't what she wanted, but she refused to give up and go home. She was ashamed to have her family—particularly her grandmother—come to see how she was misusing her talent. But she had made a contract and she stayed with the show through its run on Broadway.

One night a note came backstage saying that a man would like to see Kate. At first she thought it was one of the pranksters who delighted in taking her to a fancy restaurant, urging her to eat a great deal, and then laughing with the other fellows about it.

Instead, it was Ted Collins, of the Columbia Record Company.

Ted Collins changed Kate Smith's life. He became her manager and lifelong friend—the man who encouraged and guided her through many happy years of a singing career. Ted saw the human and spiritual qualities in Kate and knew that she had a lovely voice to give the world.

First, Ted had her make recordings for his company, then he got her a job singing in a movie theater. Later she got her big opportunity to broadcast a radio show. It wasn't long before everyone in the country was singing, "When the Moon Comes Over the Mountain," her theme song. And it was her singing of "God Bless America" that made it almost a second national anthem.

By 1940, Kate Smith was topping all radio polls in the country. When television came, Kate was one of the first to have a chance for a show.

Kate thought of those early days when audiences had laughed at her because she was so fat. On television she would be seen by millions of people. Why should she take the chance that this might happen again? She didn't need the money—radio had made her both wealthy and famous.

But Kate's courage was great, and so was her love of singing. She decided to take the challenge. At once her rich voice won the admiration of television audiences, and soon a new generation was humming her theme, "When the Moon Comes Over the Mountain."

Television viewers saw Kate Smith as a symbol of the fine things which have made this country great—generosity, good sportsmanship and goodwill towards all people.

No wonder President Franklin D. Roosevelt, when introducing her to Queen Elizabeth and King George VI, said:

"This is Kate Smith. This is America."

Chapter VIII

Al Capp

CREATOR OF LI'L ABNER

Al Capp, creator of the Li'l Abner comic strip, was born Alfred G. Caplin in 1909 at New Haven, Connecticut. He had his name changed to Al Capp because that is what everyone called him anyway.

One day, when Al was nine years old, his father gave him 50¢ to get a haircut—35¢ for the haircut, 5¢ for a tip to give the barber and 10¢ for trolley fare. But that isn't the way Al figured it. He had seen a sign in the window of a barber school in downtown New Haven which advertised haircuts for 15¢—

with *no* tipping. He hitched a ride on an ice cart to save the trolley fare. But when he hopped off in front of the barber academy, he landed right in the path of a trolley car. He was caught under the wheel and, as a result, lost his left leg.

After he got home from the hospital, Al found life wasn't too bad because everyone was so concerned about him. People who used to ignore him suddenly started bringing presents and giving him a lot of attention. But when he was fitted with a wooden leg, he had a big letdown. He went through weeks of stumbling, hurting, crying and feeling discouraged before he learned to walk. Even then he didn't walk like everyone else, as he had hoped.

But he managed.

It took Al Capp a long time to get used to living with a wooden leg. First, he had to learn to ignore the reactions of other people. Some stared at him, or looked the other way. Others changed the subject when his handicap was mentioned. Next, he was able to ignore the artificial leg, too. After all, he realized it was only a gadget, and gadgets don't always work right.

Finally, Al learned to joke about his wooden leg. He says that he has only half the chance of catching athlete's foot as most people, and he saves money on socks! He buys six pairs at a time—all alike, tacking one sock on the wooden leg, and then rotating the other eleven on his good foot.

Al was never very good at sports, so it wasn't too hard being left out of these activities. Because he couldn't spend his time playing football and baseball, it was only natural for him to do a lot with his mind and hands.

He became interested in drawing and from the beginning

his favorite drawings were cartoons. Al would talk the neighbors' daughters into posing for him. When he'd finish his pictures he let the girls look at them. Instead of the beautiful young ladies they thought they would see, they discovered that Al had drawn them, cartoon-like, with huge noses and flappy ears. Of course, he had a hard time getting the same girl to pose twice.

In his teens Al and a neighborhood friend took a trip to the Cumberland mountains in Kentucky. Meeting the natural, kindly mountain people gave Al the ideas which were later to grow into Li'l Abner cartoons.

At nineteen, Al began to take special art classes. While attending an art school in Boston, he met and married Catherine Cameron, a fellow student. It was the time of the big depression, and most people, including Al, had little money. He started going to art school three different times, but each time money problems forced him to quit.

Al went to New York where he earned $50 a week—working sixteen hours a day at cartoons he didn't like. After six months he went back to Boston with enough money saved to study at the Massachusetts School of Art.

Two years later Al Capp drew sample Li'l Abner cartoons and showed them to newspaper publishers in New York. One newspaper offered him $200 a week—if he would change Abner into the publisher's idea of "a nice, clean-cut American boy." "Nothing doing," said Al, who felt that a true creative artist doesn't work that way. Instead he took his sketches to another publisher who agreed to leave Li'l Abner the character Al had dreamed up. However, he would only receive a small fraction of the salary offered by the first publisher.

Al accepted this offer. Doing what he wanted was more important than making a big salary.

Now he does both, because Li'l Abner made Al Capp famous. His cartoons are published in hundreds of newspapers. In them, Al pokes fun at people—ordinary ones and famous ones—including high government officials. The characters in Li'l Abner represent all of us.

Some of Al Capp's cartoons hang in the Smithsonian Institution in Washington, D. C.—in honor of the man who makes people enjoy laughing at themselves, just as he learned to laugh at himself.

Chapter IX

Wilma Rudolph

THE WORLD'S SPEEDIEST WOMAN

Wilma Rudolph has been called the speediest woman in the world, but she says that she never hurries unless she is wearing track shoes. Wilma was America's star woman athlete in the 1960 Olympics in Rome.

Wilma hasn't always been a runner, or even a very good walker. A tiny, sickly baby, she was four years old before she even started to toddle. Then scarlet fever and double pneumonia struck. She was near death for weeks. She finally pulled through only to be left without the use of one leg because the infection had damaged some important nerves.

Doctors said that Wilma *might* be able to walk someday if she could get special treatment. But that treatment was available only at a clinic nearly fifty miles away from where her family lived.

Wilma's mother worked six days a week and for two years, on her day off, she took her daughter to the clinic. Often Mrs. Rudolph had to carry Wilma and every night she spent many hours massaging Wilma's legs. Wilma's older brothers and sisters helped, too.

When Wilma was six she could hop a short distance, but then her leg would give way. Two years later she was fitted with a special shoe which allowed her to limp to school.

Her first coach was her big brother, Wesley. He knew how important it was to exercise so he took a bottomless peach basket and mounted it on a pole in their backyard. Then he got a basketball and taught Wilma how to shoot baskets and how to dribble the ball while running around the backyard. Wilma did this—limping and wearing a heavy high shoe at the same time. One day her mother glanced out the window and saw Wilma running around without any shoes! Mrs. Rudolph could hardly believe her eyes.

Wilma's next coach was her high school teacher, Clinton Gray. He named her "Skeeter," short for mosquito, because she was always buzzing around so fast. Under Clinton Gray's coaching, Wilma became a star basketball player. When she graduated from high school, he helped her get into Tennessee A & I University where she became a member of the women's track team, under Coach Edward Temple.

It wasn't easy at college. She had to work four hours a day in an office. In addition, she often ran two hours a day with the track team. Yet she earned a B average in her classroom studies, and still found time for social life and dates. One of her dates was Bill Ward, whom she married in 1961.

In 1960, Wilma did the impossible. She was the first American woman to win three Olympic gold medals in track. She was voted the *No. 1 Woman Athlete of the Year* in both 1960 and 1961.

In 1961, she was named America's outstanding amateur athlete. The award was made by the Amateur Athletic Union to Wilma Rudolph as:

> **"the amateur athlete who, by performance, example, and good influence did the most to advance the cause of good sportsmanship during the year."**

Chapter X

Alec Templeton

THE MAN WHO FOUND HUMOR IN MUSIC

Two-year-old Alec Templeton climbed up on the bench of the upright piano and tried to imitate the sound of the near-by church bells. To his family's surprise, his piano church bells sounded very real.

After that, he corrected his sister if she played a wrong note while practicing her piano lesson. At four he composed a lullaby, which his

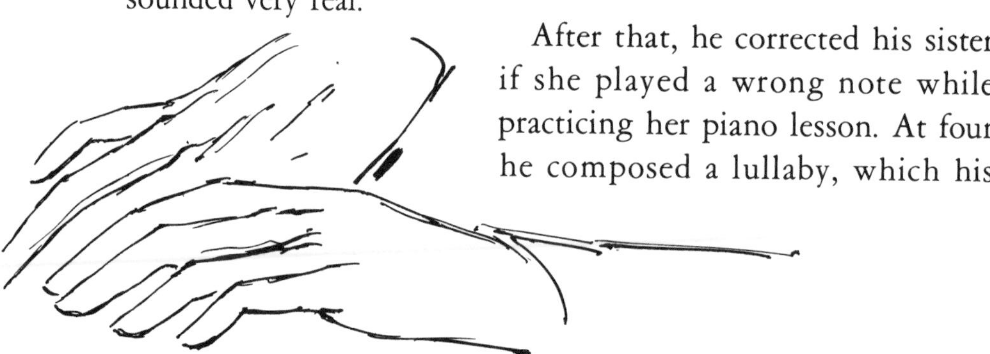

mother used to sing him to sleep. At five he directed a choir of his playmates. He wasn't bothered by the fact that his hands were too small to span all the chords in the pieces he played—he simply used his elbows.

Alec was born blind, but that didn't bother him either. In fact, he was seven years old before he found out that he was any different from his family and friends. No one waited on him. He was taught to dress himself as any child would be. His two older sisters treated him as if he had sight.

Alec was a very happy little boy. He loved to imitate the people of Cardiff, South Wales, in Britain, where he lived. He delighted in making his voice or laugh sound like theirs, and in giving speeches like some of the local politicians.

By the time Alec was seven it was clear that his musical talent was so great it must be developed. He was then taught about his blindness, and he learned the Braille system of reading, so he could study music and record the music he composed.

Alec was sent to the finest music schools in England. Soon he was receiving great honors. At the age of twelve he was given a job by the British Broadcasting Company. From then on he earned enough money and scholarships to pay for his education himself. At thirteen he won an award for composition; at sixteen he won first prize over twenty thousand other pianists in a contest.

Alec learned to play every kind of music smoothly and easily without missing a note. He learned hundreds of pieces by hearing others play, listening to phonograph records and studying Braille texts. He memorized complicated music after hearing it only a few times. In learning concertos for piano and orchestra, he had to learn the orchestra part, too, so he could play without being able to see the conductor. He was just a young man when he began giving concerts with the best orchestras in England.

All this success didn't cause Alec to take himself too seriously. He still thought the world was a very merry place. At the height of his career he began giving piano-imitations of well-known composers and concert artists. He was doing in music what the cartoonist does in drawing. This is called musical satire, and Alec used it at a time when few people had ever heard of it. His audiences roared with laughter at the imitations which were so good that the listeners could always guess who was being imitated.

Soon Alec included an entire section of humorous music into the list he was prepared to play. He played a good piano in such a way that it sounded horribly out of tune; he imitated grand opera; he played classics in a very serious manner and, in the midst of the piece, suddenly switched to swing.

In 1935 Alec Templeton came to the United States where he became a favorite on radio, in night-clubs and in concert halls. Among his many records, two favorites are: *Children's Concert* and Gershwin's *Rhapsody in Blue.*

Alec Templeton never considers that he is living or working under a handicap. He says there is fun in life and there is fun in music—all you have to do is look for it.

Chapter XI

Wendell Johnson

BECAUSE HE STUTTERED

A train couldn't leave on schedule because a young passenger stuttered so badly he wasn't able to tell the conductor where he was going. The passenger was Wendell Johnson, and it took him five whole minutes to say "Milwaukee."

Today—many years later—Wendell Johnson is an expert on speech problems and thinks nothing of making speeches to large audiences. He has given several hundred of them.

Wendell, youngest of six children, grew up on a cattle and wheat ranch in Kansas. At night the children would gather around their father to hear stories of his past adventures. He had been a real Western cowboy. During the day Wendell and his brothers and sisters helped herd the cattle. They all loved horseback riding, and Wendell always rode his horse to school.

Wendell hadn't always stuttered. At the age of five he accompanied his sister to a one-room schoolhouse where he recited a poem, without a mistake, to the older children. But when Wendell started first grade his teacher told Mr. and Mrs. Johnson that the boy was smart enough to do second grade work, if only he didn't stutter.

The Johnsons were surprised. They never noticed anything wrong with their son's speech, and neither had anyone else. Whatever the teacher was calling "stuttering," she was the only one calling it that.

But what the teacher said worried Wendell's parents, and they decided to take him to their family doctor.

The doctor didn't know what to do for stuttering (nor did anyone else fifty years ago), so he did the kindest thing he could think of. He gave Wendell sugar pills flavored with peppermint.

Of course, the pills didn't do any good.

Throughout the years many people tried to help. They would correct Wendell, or give him advice, or say the word for him when he couldn't get it out by himself. They thought they were doing the right thing. But the more fuss they made about Wendell's speech problem, the harder it became for him to speak at all.

He stuttered through high school and into college. Nothing seemed to help.

When he was twenty years old, Wendell decided to go to the speech clinic at the University of Iowa. The cat really did have his tongue the day he arrived. He just gasped when he tried to tell the girl at the desk what he wanted. Finally he got in by showing her the letter he had received from the director of the clinic, Dr. Lee Edward Travis.

Dr. Travis took Wendell to his classroom and asked him to read something to the class. He read for five minutes—and got out four words.

The clinic was beginning a program of research on stuttering, and Wendell was a member of the first group of stutterers. They gave him every kind of test imaginable. They made records of his voice, tested his muscles, took pictures of his eye movements, sat him in cold water to record his shivering, hypnotized him, and measured his breathing. They had him talk with pebbles in his mouth, with his teeth together, and in time to a metronome.

While the university was studying Wendell, he was studying, too. He learned and taught many different subjects, and worked to aid others who had speech problems. He had thought he would become a writer. Instead, he became head of the speech clinic he had gone to for help.

A great deal has been learned about the different causes of stuttering since the day Wendell Johnson's doctor gave him the peppermint pills. For instance, it is now known that all children repeat and hesitate in trying to say what they mean. This is not stuttering. It can become stuttering if people make an issue over it.

There are about one million stutterers in this country and Wendell Johnson has personally helped at least 2,500. He has helped young people with speech difficulties as well as grown-ups who have stuttered all of their lives. He has written many books and articles on this subject.

Wendell Johnson is devoting his life to a better understanding of speech problems—and it all started because he stuttered.

Chapter XII

A DIFFERENT KIND OF SUCCESS

Though many handicapped persons have achieved greatness, most of them, like most non-handicapped people, find their satisfaction in ordinary success. Typical are the stories of Bill Sweezo, a linotypist and father; Mary Kessel, a housewife and mother; and Jim Kellen, a young librarian. These three people live within a short distance of one another in Minneapolis and St. Paul, Minnesota.

BILL SWEEZO

BILL SWEEZO

Nine-year-old Bill Sweezo had been going to school for four years and he still was in the first grade.

It was because Bill was almost deaf. He could hear only half as well as other children.

Going to school was hard for Bill, and at home he was lonely, often unable to hear the chattering of his seven brothers and sisters.

Then Bill's father died of pneumonia. Bill's mother decided to send him to the state school for the deaf, where trained teachers could give him more help than he could get in their one-room country school.

"I'll never forget that day," Bill says. "I was looking out the window at our house—I did a lot of that in those days—when I saw a lady walking along the highway. She turned on the dirt road and walked into our drive."

She was the school principal, who had walked nine miles to tell Mrs. Sweezo there was a place for Bill at the state school for the deaf.

For the next month Bill eagerly looked forward to going away to school, and having his first train ride. The day finally came when a teacher took Bill and several other deaf children on the eighty-mile trip. But saying goodbye to his family wasn't easy. In fact, Bill cried all the way.

The tears changed to smiles when Bill settled down in a dormitory with nineteen other boys. The scenery was beautiful and everyone was kind and understanding. More important, Bill now had people he was learning to talk to. Carrying on a conversation was a new and exciting adventure because not being able to hear had made it difficult for him to learn to speak.

At the new school, Bill found that many of the children his age had already learned sign language and some were beginning to read lips. He knew that some day he would be able to do this, too. It was fun being one of the boys.

Bill started kindergarten again. From first grade he was skipped to third and in time he graduated from high school. During those years he had training in several trades. He took metal shop, cabinet work, tailoring and printing—the last for four years.

After graduation, he got a job at a publishing company.

Bill is still there—one of the best linotypists in the business. His fellow workers say he is fun to have around. He can't hear any better, and speaking still isn't too easy, but he can ask questions and do some lip-reading. He can write questions and read answers because he had a good education.

Bill says, "I can hear some noise in the shop—a linotype machine isn't the quietest thing in the world. I kid the other fellows that they are the ones who are handicapped, because they have to listen to all that racket."

There is a racket at home, too. Bill married a girl he met at the school for the deaf. They have three healthy children, none of whom has any problem with hearing.

The family share in many hobbies, but Bill's favorite hobby is serving other hard-of-hearing people.

MARY HICKMAN KESSEL

Mary Hickman was a high school senior that February day when she was hit by a skidding car. After six weeks in the hospital, she came home with her arm completely paralyzed. She had to wear a metal brace called an *airplane splint.* It held her arm straight out so it wouldn't slip from the shoulder socket. She wore the splint all spring and summer. When it became too cold to try to pin a coat over the bulky brace, Mary began wearing her arm in a sling.

It was her right arm that was paralyzed, and Mary had been right-handed.

She had to learn many new things. The tasks that had seemed simplest, like combing her hair and brushing her teeth, became difficult when she tried doing them with her left hand.

Mary had to learn something even harder. The accident made her very self-conscious. She thought of herself as the girl with the useless arm. She had to learn to see herself as Mary Hickman, a person.

It took Mary a long time to see herself as the courageous girl she really was. She made jokes about her arm and wore gaily colored slings to match her dresses, but she didn't really feel very gay.

As soon as she was strong enough, Mary finished high school, then started college. All the while she was in college, she was working with a therapist who tried to get some life into the paralyzed arm. For four years he massaged and stretched muscles. He managed to restore a small amount of strength to her hand. Most important, he made her realize the value of looking forward to accomplishing more in time. He taught her that any tiny achievement, even being able to hold a pen in her right hand, meant a lot.

In college, Mary swam, played golf and tennis, drove a car and did well in her studies. Still, she thought of herself as the girl with the paralyzed arm.

When Mary graduated from college she became a teacher and then a social worker. At last she realized what she really was—someone of value. For here was the girl who thought she needed help, helping others!

This was only the beginning. Mary then married Vernon Kessel and started a whole new career as a wife and later mother to two frisky boys, Greg and David.

As a homemaker, Mary does more with her one good arm than most women do with two. When she wanted built-in bookcases removed from her house, she got a crowbar and took them out. Then she discovered that there were no finished door frames behind the cases and no flooring under them. She drove to a lumber yard for material and some instructions; then she put in the door frames and fitted in the flooring. She painted her living room and dining room walls and ceilings and even wall-papered her kitchen. She sews, knits, and has gardened a 40 by 50 foot plot.

Mary Hickman Kessel now thinks of herself as being just like anyone else. But she isn't. She is just a little more generous, a little more warm-hearted and understanding than most. Perhaps the troubles she has experienced have helped to make her the fine person she is.

JIM KELLEN

When the boys at St. Thomas College in St. Paul, Minnesota, want a good book to read, they ask their librarian, Jim Kellen.

Jim was born in a small town in southwestern Minnesota. He enjoyed working with his hands—trying the things his father could do well—farming, laying bricks, wiring a house, working on a threshing crew. In high school, Jim played football and basketball and went out for track.

At the beginning of his third year, Jim became very ill with polio. He missed the rest of that school year and all of the next. But when he was strong enough to read, he would lie on his hospital bed with a book beside him. He studied everything he missed in school, and more. When he left the hospital, he took examinations and was able to return to school as a senior. Although able to attend classes only one day a week, he was graduated only a year later than had he never missed a day.

After graduation Jim went to St. Thomas College where he studied to become a teacher and librarian. His right arm is completely paralyzed. His legs are paralyzed, too, but he has the use of one hip and both feet. He will have to use a wheel chair the rest of his life. But that doesn't stop Jim Kellen. He has gone to more places, done more things and has more interests than most people.

Jim takes great pleasure in the things he does—painting, fishing, reading, and private tutoring. He can use a typewriter with his one good hand, and types 30 words a minute.

Jim drives his own car, and likes taking his friends for rides. Since his car has automatic transmission, power steering and power brakes, Jim needs almost no special equipment. He passed his driver's test on the first try, while many people have to try two or three times before they pass. He has driven with friends to Washington, D. C., New York City, Baltimore and Philadelphia. He usually drives alone on the two-hundred mile trip to his home town.

All of the people written about in this book have something in common. It is their attitude. Jim Kellen expresses it with this advice: "Don't be afraid to work and work hard, even if you get little or nothing for it. There are lots of things we should do in life without pay."

"And always remember," Jim adds, "the greatest handicaps are those not of the body, but of the will to keep trying."

About the Authors and Artist

RAVINA GELFAND in her research and interviews for *They Wouldn't Quit* discovered enough examples to fill many books. This confirmed the belief she has long had that handicapped people can and do adapt to the world around them. Mrs. Gelfand graduated from the University of Minnesota where she concentrated on English, journalism and psychology. She also did post-graduate work in English and writing at both the University and Macalester College. She is a former weekly newspaper editor and has written for radio and magazines. Mrs. Gelfand has also authored *Freedom of Religion in America* and *Freedom of Speech in America*.

LETHA PATTERSON is personally interested in the problems of the handicapped because she has a son who is mentally retarded. When the National Association for Retarded Children was founded in Minneapolis, in 1950, the Pattersons, who lived in St. Paul, found themselves deeply involved with the entire movement. Subsequently, Mrs. Patterson wrote numerous articles for medical, social welfare, and educational publications. Born and raised in Kansas, she graduated from the University of Kansas with a degree in bacteriology. Currently Mrs. Patterson is living in Muskogee, Oklahoma.

CHET SULLIVAN did the type of illustrating he enjoys most when he worked on *They Wouldn't Quit*. An experienced artist, Mr. Sullivan has had his own studio and has free-lanced for advertising agencies, publishing companies and many other clients. He has worked in Chicago and New York City in addition to the Twin Cities. During World War II he headed a group of artists to draw maps and other essential material for the photo intelligence section of the United States Air Force, where he rose to the rank of Colonel. Currently Mr. Sullivan is head artist and designer for an envelope firm, and lives in Minneapolis, Minnesota.